Faith and Favor My Mother Taught Me How to Pray

I0165588

J. WILEY-HICKS

Faith Publishing

God grant me the serenity to accept the things
I cannot change, courage to change the things I can,
and wisdom to know the difference.

This is the story of my life. It contains the joys, hurts, the happiness and pain that I have endured. I feel I must finally release and let go of all these particular situations and to share my testimony of how I made it through. I believe my story will allow someone to know that no matter what you may go through or how you perceive yourself, if you learn to have faith in God and yourself, you can and you will be a conqueror and live victoriously.

I want to dedicate this book to my wonderful mother, Betty, who has gone on to glory and her eternal rest. Her love, and the prayers that she taught me, have made me into the strong, God-fearing woman I am today.

I also want to give honor to my second mom, my mother's older sister, Mabel, who has loved and nurtured me through all my trials and tribulations. She has always been there for me, and I thank God for His blessing of providing me with two strong women of faith that gave me proper guidance and instructions in my life's walk. They both are now my guardian angels and looking after me from heaven.

Table of Contents

Chapter 1

I **ENTERED THIS** world on October 31, 1951, in Columbus, Ohio at Ohio State University Hospital.

I was born with pneumonia and was a blue baby because of the lack of oxygen in my lungs. I was always a fragile child, and my mother did a whole lot of praying that God would heal my body. From the very beginning of my life, the devil knew I was going to live and be a soldier on the battlefield for the Lord, winning souls for the kingdom of God, but even though he meant for my destruction, God did not permit his schemes to succeed.

The devil has been called the prince of this world's atmosphere, because he was cast out of heaven when he and some of the angels that followed him wanted to rule and defy God's order. God, the creator of this universe, gave him dominion over sickness, disasters, and the many calamities of this earthly realm, but he can only do what God permits him to do; he must get God's permission before he can do anything. The devil has power, but God has all power.

I was born with a purpose, as I believe each and everyone of us are; I am determined, with God's guidance, to complete my life's mission. The devil wanted to snatch me from my mother's bosom before I could become the warrior for God I was destined to be. My birthday is on Halloween, and all of my life I have been teased and taunted because I have always had a special aura of mysteriously being able to sense things before they happened.

My maternal grandmother Isabelle said I was born with a veil over my face; this means having a natural gift of being able to know what is going to occur before it does.

Chapter 2

I **DON'T CLAIM** to be a soothsayer or a psychic, but I believe I have a prophetic calling, and I am learning to develop this gift more by tuning into God's voice and listening in the spirit for His instructions. This pagan holiday is known as the night of the dead, where spirits are supposed to rise and cause horrific things to happen. I have never been afraid of what this day represents. As a child and on into my adult life, I celebrate this day of my birth. Everything happens for a purpose, and I believe my being born on this particular day also has a reason in God's eyes. The day is celebrated by people in different cultures, but it represents to me a time for the little children to dress in costumes of their choice and go door to door asking for candy, or as it is better known, trick-or-treat. The pumpkins get decorated as jack o' lanterns with scary faces or smiling funny faces. I preferred my children to attend a private party which included games and bobbing for apples, but they still wanted to go through the neighborhood with family and friends.

My mother had other holiday babies as well. My brother Wayne was born on April 1st, known as April Fools' Day; my youngest sister, Iona was born the day after Christmas—my mother went into labor with her on Christmas, but she came the next day. The year my youngest brother, Kevin, was born, his birthday fell on Labor Day.

My mother had eight children, but she lost a son during his birth.

Chapter 3

MY FATHER, ROBERT, was my mother's first husband. They divorced when I was just two years old.

My two older brothers, Larry and Mike, loved their little sister, and since I was sickly, they were always very protective of me.

I had problems with breathing and chronic bronchitis, but I still would do things to get on their nerves. They spoiled me anyway, because I was their baby sister. They were great brothers. I was a skinny little girl growing up; I never had many friends, but I had a passion for reading. I guess I was considered a bookworm, because I was always reading. I felt there was knowledge in learning, so I would read many books on every subject; I wanted to be smart, since I didn't think I was beautiful.

I will begin my story telling about the situations that have influenced and molded me into the person I am today. I give respect and much love to the two people that birthed me. My father was a man of great intelligence with a business mind, and he had a gift of gab and persuasion. He had a degree in Civil Engineering; I remember going to classes with him at OSU when I was young and meeting the professors. I enjoyed going because after class we would go get some butter pecan ice cream or his favorite hamburgers, White Castle burgers.

He was an entrepreneur and owned several construction

companies. He served in the military, the Army and Navy during World War II, and was even in a Hollywood movie. He played one of the main characters, a detective looking for leaders of a drug cartel.

I went to visit my father in California; at that time he lived in Baldwin Hills. This was a beautiful suburban area on the outskirts of Los Angeles, where many celebrities and movie stars lived. Every home had a swimming pool, and my dad even had a banana tree in his cultured, landscaped yard. Palm trees lined the streets. This was like a place you only dream about, but I really experienced it. My dad lived close to Ike and Tina Turner, and their kids would come over and play with my dad's stepchildren. Ray Charles and Robert Stack were neighbors as well. My dad wanted me to stay and wait till Ray Charles came off tour so he could arrange for me to have an audition. I was fifteen at the time. I stayed in California for a few months and was going to school in Watts, training to become a dental assistant.

This community had been destroyed by some of its own angry residents; there were torn-down buildings and evidence of burned stores and properties, because of racial disparity in the early 1960s.

My dad tried to convince me to stay, but I was homesick, so I decided to come back to Ohio.

I never got that audition with Ray Charles; I passed up a once in a lifetime opportunity, to return home.

My dad started another business venture and moved to the State of Washington, after I came back to Ohio.

Chapter 4

I **HAVE OFTEN** wondered what might have transpired and how my life would have been different if I had stayed. My dad was an accomplished pianist. He couldn't sing, though; he jokingly told me that when he was in school, the music teachers gave him a grade of an A for not singing. There was another side to my father, because he had an insatiable craving for fame and fortune and wanted them more expediently than his businesses allowed, so he resorted to criminal activity.

He was not a small time con man but was a highly intelligent organizer of many illegal plans that brought him hundreds of thousands of dollars and beautiful homes, fancy cars, and women—only to lose it all and spend the majority of his life in and out of federal prisons.

My father was involved in many crimes, including masterminding major bank heists, counterfeiting rings, drug trafficking, and much more. He was like a godfather of the Black Mafia. The last crime he was involved in was a very bad drug transaction; the men there were planning to rob and kill him, but when it was over, he survived, and there were fatalities, and he was sentenced to thirty years in prison. Through a lot of legal ramifications and years of appeals he was able to be released from prison on a presidential pardon. The President of the United States allowed my father's sentence to be commuted. He was in critical condition because of progressive kidney failure.

Chapter 5

THE DOCTORS ONLY gave him six months to live. I was willing to give one of my kidneys to him, but he was not a good candidate for this surgery because of his age and other health issues. He had to receive dialysis treatments three times a week. He moved back to Ohio be with his family. He said this was the richest time of his life, being able to impart wisdom and knowledge to his grandchildren, especially the grandsons who were old enough to understand all the glamour of the lifestyle that he had lived could bring, but he wanted them not to follow in his footsteps and to learn from his mistakes and to achieve their goals by getting their education and to be patient, not to get sidetracked and move too quickly.

He encouraged them to strive to be law-abiding citizens, because their dreams and visions could become reality with hard work and a creative business mind, without the drama of having to be arrested and face life behind prison walls for trying to beat the system. I was a daddy's girl, so it was not hard to forgive his errors and mistakes; I can really say I had a father that would do anything for me. He would have given me the world if he could, and there were many good and positive things about my dad.

I write poetry, and I wrote a poem for my dad when I was about twelve years old. He was so proud, and he always encouraged me to express my feelings in writing.

I remember my dad came to church to hear me sing. He said I had a voice like my mother's. He was so amazed that I had such a strong voice coming out of such a little girl. He had tears in his eyes as I sang my song.

I know I have written so much pertaining to my father, but I had to release the good and bad memories, because there were inner demons in my father that those many years of being in prison had caused. He spoke on unnatural thoughts of perversion and incest which almost destroyed our father and daughter relationship. I felt sorry for my dad; I knew he didn't understand how much this sickness affected my mental and emotional state. I tried to tell him on several occasions and to convince him this illicit act would never happen, but as much as I tried to tell him it was wrong and hurtful, his thoughts remained warped for many years.

I was able to witness to my father about God's love and forgiveness before he died, and I believe he asked God's forgiveness for all his wrongdoings. I knew he had changed his way of thinking, because he told me when I was going through rough times in my marriage, instead of fighting, I should pray and let God lead me away from this abusive relationship. Although the doctors in prison had only given him a short time to live, he defied the odds and lived about two more years than expected. I was at work when I got a call from the hospital that my dad's heart had stopped while he was on his dialysis treatment.I met my brother Mike at the hospital and the doctors told us Dad was brain dead, but they would keep him on life support for a few days. It was not our decision but theirs, so I had asked them to let us have till that Sunday, which was in two days because I wanted to be there when they took him off the life support machine, and they agreed.

On that Sunday morning, my sister Denise went with me to the hospital.

I wanted to pray and have church with him in the hospital room during his last hours.

We were praying and asking God's mercy. My sister said she believed he had made his peace with God. My dad was seventy five years old when he died. I may not be proud of all his life decisions, but I will always love my father and I believe I will see him again when our family gathers for that great reunion in the sky.

Chapter 6

Now, it is time to tell of the person who most influenced my life. These stories revolve around the wonderful mother I had. It is because of her loving spirit and faith in God and the many prayers she prayed for me and with me that I have overcome. My mother taught me how to pray and to believe that I could do all things through Christ which strengthens me.

My mother married twice after her divorce from my father. She had four children with my dad: my older brother Terry died at birth; and then there was Larry, James Michael, and yours truly. Although my brother's first name was from our maternal grandfather, he always was called Michael or Mike. Mom had four children with her second husband: my brother Wayne, who was born with blonde hair and blue eyes, just like our mom when she was a baby, which caused her to win first place in the baby contest at the Pumpkin show in Circleville.

Wayne was so cute and always in mischief. He had problems when he was born because he was born with water on the brain; doctors told my mom she should consider putting him in an institution because he could possibly have retardation and not be able to function normally as he grew up. She told them she would never hospitalize him. She went on a prayer vigil, fasting and praying for his complete healing, and God answered her prayers; the only institution he would ever be in was a college, from which he would graduate and receive an accounting degree. He was another miracle child from God.

My sister Marla was the next to be born. She always remained me of Shirley Temple, the child actress, because her hair was curly and she had those same cute dimples, and she always had an older spirit than the age she really was. As a youngster, she was raised by her father's mother. Her grandmother's name was Marybul, but her grandchildren called her Mim; my sister lived there for years, but I always wanted her home, and I would cry when she would visit and then had to leave. I could not understand why she didn't live with us, but it was better for her to be in a small town and get her education and help her grandmother. She learned to cook and crochet and so many other useful things. She did come home to live with us after she was older, and she was so polite and well mannered.

My sister Iona was born about three years after Marla. She was such a beautiful baby, and as she grew up, she had a flair for fashion. She kept her hair and clothes impeccable, and she was very popular and classy. As the baby girl she was of course spoiled, but then came my brother, Kevin; he was a cute baby and he always got his way because he was the youngest, Mom's baby boy. He was good in sports, running track and playing football, and he married his high school sweetheart, Lisa. They are still married after more than twenty-five years, with three sons and a beautiful daughter.

Chapter 7

MY SIBLINGS' FATHER who was my first stepfather was a businessman, a barber by trade; he owned his shop on the Hilltop, which was on the west side of Columbus. He also worked for a juvenile facility as a youth leader. He was a well dressed man, and he was very intelligent. He was an excellent cook and knew how to prepare gourmet meals; he had worked as a chef at Ohio State University many years before he had his own business. He was a disciplinarian and he was harsh in the way he disciplined my brother, Wayne; he ruled with an iron fist and a razor strap.

I always felt sorry for him because it seemed he was always getting a whipping, it seemed he could not do the right thing to measure up to his father's expectations for one thing or another, but my brother said it made him grow up respectful of his elders, and he never was in trouble in school or with the law. My brother would work at the barber shop, sweeping up hair and cleaning, and this taught him a good work ethic at an early age.

Chapter 8

GROWING UP, I had an inferiority complex. I didn't feel I was part of the family, because I was not treated kindly and shown love like my younger brothers and sisters, because I was the stepchild. I felt unwanted and unloved. I had pain and heartache, I wanted so hard to be accepted. My brothers and sisters were taught by their dad that I was their half sister; they didn't understand, so they would tell their friends that I was not a whole sister. As they became older, they began to realize we were from the same mother so how could we not be real brothers and sisters? My older brothers were not living with us, because as soon as my brother Larry was of age, he joined the military; he was only sixteen, and my brother Mike went to live with our great aunt Maude.

My mom expressed love to all her children, but I went through a lot of mental anguish and was scarred emotionally as a child. Mom told me my stepdad had been mistreated as a child by his mother's husband, so I don't think he really knew how to relate to stepchildren. At that time he only showed love to his own children. There were times when he would buy treats and I was not asked to have any. I would go to my room and cry, because I was not shown the same treatment as my brothers and sisters. Later on down the years, I was able to establish a relationship with my stepfather, and he even gave me words of wisdom and encouragement when I was grown and going through problems in my life. I had two children at that time, and they looked on him as a grandfather. My oldest son became a barber and hair stylist after following his advice. He was a good man and he loved his children very much; my mother was with him for many years, but then my younger siblings had to suffer and go through the experience and pain of divorce, as I had, only they were older, so this breakup between their parents affected them in even a more detrimental way.

I have always loved my younger brothers and sisters with my whole heart. They were too young to understand what I went through growing up. They were children and didn't know any better. I grew up protecting them, whether it was helping with homework, beating up bullies, or keeping them out of trouble, I was there for them, and now that we are older, we have a love and appreciation that our mom instilled in us. We have built a strong relationship between us.

The problems I encountered during this time in my life established and helped build my character. These struggles made me believe in myself and gave me the strength to endure, and no matter what obstacles I had to face, I would come out a winner. I just needed to tell of this part of my life to let everyone know that if you go through divorce or separation and then remarry, you must communicate and have an understanding with the new partner, and if there are children involved, their feelings must be taken into consideration and all effort must be made to unite the two families into one.

Our mother taught us to love each other and not show a difference in our feelings for each other, because we all came from her womb, and that is what made us brothers and sisters.

Chapter 9

HER PRAYER LIFE was strong and powerful; she was an anointed prayer warrior. She touched the lives of so many people and to know her was to love her. She always made sure we had clean clothes, although we had hand-me-downs and some of our clothes came from thrift stores and other community organizations that helped low income families. My mother was a proud woman and she taught us to appreciate what we had, because she would say there is always someone in worse condition than yourself, so we were taught to appreciate what we had and to take care of our things.

We loved our mom's cooking; no matter what she fixed, it was always good, and even sometimes when we had to eat food made from government commodities—this was food that consisted of canned meat either pork or beef, powered eggs, milk, flour, butter and cheese, which was given free to families that were below a certain poverty line and income, before government food stamps were issued. I was in the Girl Scouts as a Brownie, and I was selling cookies for our troop. The cookie sales were going real good. My mom would help me and would let me go in our neighborhood after school to get orders from our neighbors.

One day I came home from school and my mom was there, but she was not herself. She couldn't walk or talk. I was so scared and began to cry because there was something so very wrong. She had taken a tablet of paper and she was able to write instructions on what was to be done. She told me in a note where the money was for the Girl Scout cookies we had sold, and she told me to help take care of my younger brothers and sisters because she had to go away to a hospital. I later learned she had a nervous breakdown. She was going through a lot of personal problems and the stress became too much, so she had to go get treatment for depression.

She was not gone long and when she came home, she was the same loving person she had always been. Her faith did not waver, and she prayed until she was healed completely and she became even stronger in her belief, and she never went back to a hospital or took medicine again for any mental disorder. Through every obstacle and situation she ever went through, she was a living testimony on the power of prayer.

We lived on the west side of town; growing up we lived in what was known as the Bottoms. It was a poor neighborhood, but it wasn't considered the ghetto. All the families got along. It didn't matter about what color you were; we looked out for each other. We were friendly with all our neighbors, especially the older people. My mom would help in any way she could by going to the grocery store or helping them with their everyday chores.

Chapter 10

I REMEMBER PRESIDENT John Kennedy had a motorcade come down West Broad Street, right past our houses, when he visited Columbus. We were all waving and shouting; we felt proud to be Americans.

Later we moved further west to the Hilltop, and my mom started going back to church. We began to attend Bible Way church, a small holiness church. Our pastor was an anointed young minister. We were some of the first members at the church and when our pastor got married my sisters Denise and Iona were the flower girls in their beautiful church wedding. Bishop and Mother Lewis had six children and have now been married over fifty years. God blessed our church, and the membership began to really show increase. My mother was a devotional praise leader, and when she sang, you could feel the presence of the Lord and the anointing in the service.

I was only nine years old when I got saved and gave my life to the Lord. I was going to a professional dance studio at that time; I was taking ballet, tap, and modern dance. My sister Denise and I were getting ready for a recital and I had started going to choir rehearsal because I also wanted to sing.

The choir director, Evangelist Trent, told me I could not keep coming to choir practice late after dance class because I was disturbing the rehearsal, and even though I would pay fines for being late, she said I had to make a decision that I was either going to dance or I was going to sing for the Lord. I chose the later.

Chapter 11

MY MOM MABEL, was really upset at first because she had paid a lot of money for me to go to dance school. I know there was quite an expense--the cost of the lessons, the dancing attire, and dance shoes. I loved her and didn't want to disappoint her, but I knew I wanted to be in the choir more than dance. I asked mom Mabel to come to church to hear me sing .I was singing a solo that Sunday and when she heard me, and seen how sincere I was at such a young age to want to serve the Lord, she started coming to our church, and before long, she gave her life to the Lord.

Daddy Jack, her husband, followed later and dedicated his life to the Lord, although at first he had told Mom he didn't want any part of church, but he heard God's voice and he answered His call.

I thank God that through them seeing how God was using me to be a witness and proclaiming the gospel at my young age, they knew that this was real. I have always said for everyone I bring to church and God saves them, I would have jewels in my crown when I get to heaven for those souls. Mom Mabel became a church missionary and Daddy Jack was appointed a deacon and also was a financial advisor on the church board. My choir director became close to my mother like a sister, and from that time on she became known to our family as Aunt Dollie.

I enjoyed being in church and I was chosen to be our youth delegate to the National Youth Convention in Washington, DC, when I was about eleven years old. It was an exciting time for me and I took pictures of our nation's Capitol and the Lincoln Memorial and other historical landmarks in Washington, DC.

Our church had a drama ministry, and we would do biblical productions. I once played the angel Gabriel in a Christmas play at our church. I learned the scriptures and recited them by heart exactly as the verses were written in the Bible, I had scenes in the play where I spoke to Elizabeth, the mother of John the Baptist and proclaiming to the Virgin Mary, about her becoming the mother of Jesus, foretelling of the birth of the Messiah, the savior of the world, God's only begotten son. I was very active as a youth in the church, and I used my gift of writing poetry for our Sunday school programs. I was always very involved in all our church activities. I would bring my friends to church, and I always tried to set an example for my friends to let them know I was a Christian and lived my life-giving honor to God and was not ashamed of allowing God to be the head of my life.

I started pulling away and began losing interest as I started getting older; in my teen years I was not letting God lead and direct my life, so I strayed away. I wanted to do things like other girls my age. I was on a basketball team at the community recreation center, and we played well. We would play other girls from different centers and we made it to the city finals, although we didn't take first place. I felt I was missing out on all the fun things my friends were doing.

Chapter 12

I STARTED TO be incorrigible. I was moving too fast, and I became permissive with certain boys, not realizing I was headed for self-destruction. We would have house parties; the parents would be in another part of the house, so sometimes we were not chaperoned properly, and the parties would get out of hand, with too much touching and kissing. I seemed to attract older boys; they could be very persuasive in getting what they wanted, and no was not in their vocabulary. I was not secure in myself during the first couple years after becoming a teenager. I felt someone cared if they called you a few times, but I found out the hard way that once they talked you into things you really didn't want to do, the phone calls stopped coming.

I built up the wrong kind of reputation, one I was not proud of. I was a tease, and that got me in a lot of trouble. My name was spoken for all the wrong reasons. My mother took me downtown to the Juvenile Detention Center for being unruly. I remember she only wanted a counselor to talk to me and put a little fear into me what could happen if I didn't obey my parents, but I got a real scare because I was kept there for a week and I started to realize that I didn't want to end up in a place like this and get branded as an incorrigible, undisciplined teen. I was fifteen at the time.

The other girls I was in with had more experience in dealing with being locked up. They tried to get me in trouble, since I didn't know the game of coping. I was actually in a couple of fights because I had to prove I was not afraid and I had to defend my self-respect when a girl gave me unwanted advances. She touched my leg while we were watching television and said something that was not acceptable to my character, so I knocked her out of her chair and had to go to isolation, but this type of incident never came up again while I was there.

My mom never gave up on me and she kept praying for me.

The day came when I had to go before the juvenile magistrate. Both my moms were there and when they presented my case, I begin to cry so hard, and told them I had learned my lesson and I wanted to go home. Both my moms were crying too, and the magistrate said he would give me a chance to prove I wanted to do right and change, so he agreed to release me. I went home, and I did do better. I told everyone that would listen, "Don't get caught up in not doing right. Obey your parents, study hard in school, and do not resort to crime, because once you're behind those bars and someone else has the authority to tell you when to wake up, when to eat and then what time to go to bed, it's no joke and life takes on a whole new meaning."

I didn't like that part of my life, and I was determined not to allow myself ever to get that out of hand and have to go back, and I never did.

Chapter 13

MY FAVORITE PASTIME as I was growing up was listening to music. One night it was late and my mom had told me to turn off the radio and go to sleep, but I was hardheaded so I put the radio under my pillow so she wouldn't hear it. It was the middle of the night and when I woke up I smelled something burning and I jumped up out of bed and my pillow was stuck to the radio and the radio was melted into the pillow and the pillow where I laid my head was burned and black.

I ran downstairs and screamed for my mom, and when she came upstairs and saw the damage and knew what could have happened, she just fell on her knees and began to cry and pray. I was upset and shaken, but I realized I had just received a miracle and even through my disobedience, God let me know I was special to Him, and He didn't allow me to lose my life or our house to be lost. It is only through His grace and mercy that I am alive today to tell this amazing story.

I was beginning to understand that God had given me my anointed mother for a reason; I was going to need every prayer she had deposited on my life in order to ward off the attacks of the devil that would come against me, and even though I would fall, I had a safety net of the Holy Spirit and I would get up again and again, because when you are down to your lowest, the only thing to do is get back up and stand.

The fact is when I became a mother, I was able to draw strength and make an impact from some of the same experiences I went through earlier.

Chapter 14

I **KNEW IT** was the prayers she prayed and taught me to pray that have got me through every situation. I have instructed my own children and grandchildren to "push" (pray until something happens) and it will; just learn to hold on to your faith, and it will come to pass. Now as I continue about my mom, I know the things she taught me are embedded in me. The scripture says train a child up in the way they should go, and they will not depart from it. This means even when they don't do as they are supposed to do, they will know right from wrong, and when they get tired of unnecessary problems which they have brought on themselves, they will remember what they were taught as a child.

My second stepfather was a hard worker at a steel mill. He treated us all good, and although he would drink, he never disrespected us. Mr. Clayton was from Georgia and he was an excellent cook. He would make Southern-style dishes that we all came to love; a lot of the dishes we didn't know what they were, but they tasted delicious. When my mom and he were dating, they would go to the horse tracks and I would babysit my brothers and sisters. I would get rewarded when they came home with the best and biggest burger from Green Gables Restaurant.

Chapter 15

MY BROTHER LARRY was still in the service. He had been in the Vietnam war. He was in the army and was a paratrooper. He had called home and told Mom he was in a military hospital for malaria and he was being sent home soon. My mom had asked me to call and find out what was going on. When I called, I found out my brother was also being treated for drug abuse; there were so many of our soldiers coming home from this war with physical and mental disabilities from the aftermath of war. Mom had got so upset that she began to cry and shake; at this time I took my mom into her bedroom to have a private and informational talk about drugs and their effects on a person. I was grown and my younger brothers and sisters were growing up and she needed to know the signs to determine if they were using or trying any kind of drugs. Mom thanked me for this conversation and the lesson on this subject.

My brother came home from the war and he told us of the horrible conditions they had to endure when they were in those fox holes, seeing their comrades get shot and die next to them. He was not the same as he was before he left. This experience made him have nightmares and wake up talking in his sleep about the war. This was frightening to us, and we tried to reach out to him and understand what he had gone through. My brother later went on to be a long-haul truck driver, and he would be on the road for weeks at a time, but he enjoyed going to different states and meeting new people. Larry was very loving and sensitive, and he loved us all so much. He would bring us presents or give us money if we cleaned up the bathtub after he was finished; even after we had children, he would do them the same way.

We all loved our brother, but we would tease him about being worrisome and always getting on our nerves. My mom was glad my brother was out of the war. It had really affected him, but it could have been worse if not for her prayers and faith. He would have Mom take care of his money; then he would worry her about getting it back until all of it was gone.

Chapter 16

MY MOM AND stepdad had bought a home, and Mom enjoyed spending time with her sister Daisy and her husband. Aunt Daisy and her husband lived in London, Ohio and when they came to town, they would come over and spend a lot of time together. My aunt Daisy was a lot of fun; she was gorgeous and had long black hair and a beautiful skin color that showed her Indian ancestry. She had eight children, and my cousins were always around when we were growing up. We had a lot of big family gatherings and reunions. Aunt Daisy died from an asthma attack. She was alone at home when this tragedy occurred. She was a woman of God and a prayer warrior, and she lived her life to the fullest and always had a kind word and a beautiful smile that was contagious.

Her funeral was an anointed church service. We praised God for another saint going home to be with the Lord.

Chapter 17

MOM WAS WORKING as a quality control inspector at the same job she had when my oldest son was born. He was now seven years old. She was never really sick, although I remember she had migraine headaches when we were growing up. It was summer and my two children, James and Pam, were visiting their paternal grandmother who lived in New Jersey. Mom told me she missed them and she was going to come over to my house that week so we could call them. She wanted to talk to them; she only had three grandchildren at that time: my son and daughter and my nephew, Mike (my brother Mike's son).

One Tuesday, I got a call that she had taken sick and she was being rushed to the hospital. When I got to the emergency room, they were transferring her to another hospital that had a trauma ward and was better equipped to treat her, because after running several tests it was conclusive that she had a stroke. The family gathered at the hospital and we all were praying that she would be healed. Mom was just forty-seven years old and we didn't want to believe she would leave us at such a young age. She was in the hospital about a week before the angels came to escort her to glory.

I worked at Ohio Bell Phone Company as a long-distance operator. Someone called from the hospital to say that my mom had gone into a semi coma. I worked downtown close to the hospital. I left work and ran all the way to the hospital. I went to her room and took her hand to let her know I was there. She opened her eyes and she took a deep breath, like a gasp of air. I believe that was her last breath. At that same time, the nurse came in the room and said I had to go out because they had to do some medical procedures on her.

I left her room and got on the phone to tell the family to come back to the hospital. Everyone began to arrive and later they let us go up to her room. She was in ICU, but they allowed all of us in. I knew something was not right because they never permit that many in a room. They had her on life support; they said she was not breathing on her own, and only the machine was causing her to live.

I felt her feet and they were very cold. I knew she was already making her transition. The family stayed for a long time, talking and consoling each other, praying for a miracle.

Mom Mabel had asked her when she first went to the hospital if she wanted her to call our pastor. I remember Mom Betty told her there was no need; I believe she knew her assignment here was finished, she had fought a good fight and was about to receive her reward for a job well done. Mom Mabel told us that evening we should go home and try to get some rest; if there was any change, they would call us.

I couldn't leave, so I stayed and everyone left, but there was something down in my spirit that made me felt my mom's spirit of life was leaving and I wanted to be there when she crossed over. I went to the chapel to pray, and while I was on my knees, I heard a voice so clear to me saying "Be strong." I knew then it was the voice of God preparing me and strengthening me for the younger siblings that would need my love and comfort in the time of our bereavement.

Just after midnight, I was in the waiting room with my cousin, Louella, who is like a sister to me, and my brother-in-law, Mike, who both had come after everyone left to be there with me. We were talking when the call came from the ICU unit. They had called for my cousin David, who is a minister, because they thought he was her son. I picked up the phone and told them I was her daughter and I would come.

I went up to the fourth floor and I was met by the doctor and nurse and they told me she had died.

I asked to see her, but they said I had to wait because they had to prepare her and then they would allow the family some time after that. The doctors told us later, if had she had lived she would had been in a vegetative state for the rest of her life. I know Mom would not want to live and be a burden, and if she could not be herself, I believe she asked God to just let her come home to glory.

I was walking to the elevator from ICU, getting ready for the family to return to the hospital, and as I walked and prayed, I heard her angelic voice. She was singing one of her praise songs that she used to sing for our church's devotional service. The title was called "You can't make me doubt Him, I know too much about Him," and I knew God was letting me know everything was alright. I remember my youngest brother took our mom's death the hardest. He kept asking God what he had done. No matter how we tried to console him, he was lost without Mom. He had been her baby, and now he had to learn to go on without her. He was only twelve or thirteen when Mom passed. He was angry with God; he didn't understand why she had to leave us. He could not talk to anyone about the pain he felt and this suffering he kept inside even as he grew to be an adult. This caused him to have an estranged relationship with God until he was finally able to realize God did not make a mistake when He called our mother home. Her work here on earth was done, and she was called to her eternal rest.

Chapter 18

THE YEARS OUR mother was with us were truly a blessing. She loved and believed in her children and told us to always give our best, but the main thing I remember about my mother is that she would always pray, and she taught each of us to pray. She taught me the power of prayer and that prayer changes things.

I liked school and would try to excel in all my studies. I was a good student and was active in sports as well. I played basketball and ran track. I was in the city Junior Olympics, and I ran unattached, which meant I was not with a particular school or team. I was really good in the broad jump, hurdles, and relays. There were coaches scouting for potential future Ohio State College athletic students. I was only fifteen, so I got a lot of attention and was noted in the paper as an upcoming track star. Then I found out I was pregnant, and my life changed.

I was afraid of making my mom and family ashamed, because teen pregnancy was frowned upon and unacceptable. It was very different, not like in today's society; although teen pregnancy is still taboo, there are more resources and agencies geared toward assisting the young, inexperienced parents. I was not going to have my baby--I felt I wasn't ready to take on such a responsibility--but after a lot of soul searching and praying, I decided I would not have an abortion.

Later in life, under different circumstances, I subjected myself to this procedure, and I have never forgotten the decision. There have been times when I wished I could turn back the hands of time.

I asked God's forgiveness for this awful act that I allowed by self to be talked into. I should have made the choice on my own, but I let my partner make the ultimate decision, telling me this was the only way. Any woman who is facing an unwanted pregnancy, you should not choose to abort the baby, allow that child a life. If you can't care for the child, don't be ashamed to make a decision to give the child up for adoption, because there are so many loving individuals that can't have a child, that will take the baby and give your child the life he or she deserves.

I remember the first trimester, the morning sickness, tiredness, always wanting to sleep and I stayed hungry, but the first time my baby kicked, I knew that whatever I didn't know about being a mom, I was willing to learn through trial and error.

My baby's daddy didn't run away or neglect his duties as a young teen father, and his stepping up to take on his share of the responsibilities made it easier to accept my pregnancy. Our beautiful baby boy, James Anthony, was born on October 9, 1967. He was premature--he only weighed four pounds and eight ounces--but to me he was perfect.

I mentioned earlier that when I was in California with my dad, he had wanted me to stay and audition for Ray Charles. He said I had the opportunity of a lifetime to give my baby everything he could ever need, but I didn't listen because I wanted my son to be raised by his mom and dad, so this was the reason I came back to Ohio.

Chapter 19

I DID LOVE to sing, and my son's father and I sung together as a duo. We were really popular locally in our hometown, and we even got to sing at the Veteran's Memorial downtown. This is the same place where many famous entertainers and stars have come to perform when they were in our city.

Sometimes, our dreams don't happen exactly as we think they should; there may be other plans that will materialize, but never give up on yourself, because in the end, you can still achieve your dreams and goals in life. My mom forgot about the shame I had caused her by having a baby out of wedlock. She became the proud grandmother of her first grandchild, the cutest little baby boy in the world. She nick-named him Tony because his middle name was Anthony. He had his dad's first name, James, but I gave him my youngest brother's middle name.

My mother worked at Ross Laboratory, the plant where they made Similac baby formula, so I was fortunate that she could get it at a discount; this really helped us to provide for his care. He was so adorable, and very smart. He began walking at nine months, and he learned everything so quickly. He was potty trained early as well. My mom watched him when I went to night school to continue my high school studies. The school district did not allow teen mothers to return to regular high school. James would work during the day to provide for our son's care and went to school at night to finish his high school education. He was proud of his son and he paid for everything, and I did not have to be a young mother that had to go on welfare. Older adults said we were good parents. I always made sure he was clean and dressed properly. It was a learning process for the both us. We wanted him to grow up knowing we felt he was a blessing and not a mistake. We were young, but God allowed us to mature and grow up with our son.

James and I married on October 5, 1968. I was sixteen and he was seventeen. Little Jimmy, as he was called, was about to turn a year old, and I was pregnant with our second child. We planned a wedding with the assistance of our family. My Aunt Dollie made me a beautiful wedding gown of lace and hand-stitched pearls, and he wore a tuxedo. We had an awesome reception with great food and a three-tiered wedding cake. All of our friends and family were there to help us celebrate our big day. They were all happy that we had made a decision to marry and make a life for our children. We went through a lot of difficulties, but we were determined to make our marriage work.Our beautiful daughter, Pamela Michelle was born February 18, 1969, four months after we were married. We tried to imitate older adults on how to be good parents, but we were so young; there were many mistakes, but we really did try to beat the odds that were against us.

Chapter 20

WE MOVED TO New Jersey and was living with his mother for a while, but we both began to have different interests and were growing apart. It was because of our age that we never did really understand all the responsibilities that went with being married. We both broke our vows and were unfaithful to each other, and our life together was not happy.

It was during this time I became involved in a relationship and fell in love with another man. I was not ashamed of my feelings or actions, and although we were not of the same race, we shared the same interests. This relationship lasted for many years, and even though we would never marry, there was a special bond between us. He was a school teacher from New Jersey, and we had met while he was vacationing and working at a friend's ice cream shop. When we looked at each other for the first time, there was an instant spark that later grew into fireworks when we touched for the first time. I never met his parents, but I had the opportunity to speak to them on many occasions. They were fine people and I did not feel they made a difference because I was not of the same race. He was of Armenian descent and his parents had been mistreated in their country before they came to the United States. I tried to understand what they had gone through and realized they knew of prejudice too, and not being accepted because they were different.

Years later when his parents died, even though I was not there in person, he knew I was with him in spirit; I was just a phone call away and I was praying for him and his family for God to comfort him during his bereavement and for his loss of his loved ones. When I lost my mom, he was there encouraging me to continue to write my poetry. I even wrote a poem for him. I would write to help my depression and the domestic violence I went through. There were times when I was going through my mental episodes and was hospitalized that I would feel he was there with me, and I think it was at that low point of my life that he came through as a true friend. It would be years later before I would see him again, and this was after my divorce.

We had decided I would come to Philadelphia for a few days to visit. I was so excited and when I saw him at the airport we knew the feelings we had shared so long ago was still there and we would always know that what we had was real. Those few days together were some of the happiest times of my life. We didn't make any promises to each other about our future; we just enjoyed the moment with no regrets. This was a time in my life, in my early twenties, that I can never forget, and this is a part of me that kept me going and able to face other disappointments and failed relationships.

Chapter 21

ALTHOUGH I HAD many relationships throughout my life, there are only a few that have really impacted my life. My first marriage ended after six years. We had allowed the disagreements and bitter arguments and fights to take their toll, and we both knew we had to stop the unhappiness. Neither of us wanted our children to suffer and grow up in a home where the love between their parents had diminished, and we just did not want to keep living a lie. I want to say that I feel a man and woman should not stay together for the sake of the children, because in the long run there will be more damage than just getting out of the relationship and rebuilding your life so that you can be instrumental in the development of your children's lives.

I was a single mom for many years and for many reasons. I dated and had relationships, and each had its own unique quality and persona. I dated a doctor for a few months who was a child psychologist. He showed me a lot of fun times. We were not looking to be in a serious and committed relationship, so we just went out and enjoyed each other's company. We decided to go out of town one night just to get out of the city; we visited another doctor friend of his and rode around in his Rolls Royce for the evening. I later dated a lawyer for quite a while and we would exercise and run a mile every day, early in the morning before he had to go to court on his cases. I would sometimes go to the law library with him when he had to gather information on particular briefings pertaining to certain cases. We were in a serious relationship and had even talked about marriage, but in the end we parted as friends. He later married someone else and eventually divorced, after which he moved out of state and we lost contact.

I have dated business owners, working men, and even a few playboys, but as I searched to find myself, I was not completely satisfied or fulfilled in any of these relationships.

I thought that one day I would find happiness, but until then I just went through life enjoying whatever it had to offer.

Chapter 22

MY OLDEST SON is still my pride and joy. He is intelligent and still hand-some; he has many God-given talents. He is a musician; his dad taught him to play the guitar when he was about nine years old. He composes and writes his own lyrics and music, and his instrument of choice is his bass guitar. He has battled many personal demons, especially addiction to drugs, mainly crack cocaine. The devil used to tell me my son would never be off crack. I kept praying, and even when things looked like they were getting worse, I believed the promise of God and I told the devil he was a liar, and my son would be delivered from drugs and have his own testimony on how the power of prayer and trusting in God brought him through.

God has a calling on his life, and he has begun to walk into his destiny and purpose. He has a way to go, but he must realize it's already been worked out and he shall come forth as pure gold. He has always been an excellent learner. He was in the scholastic achievement book of *Who's Who of High School Students* while he was attending school in Mountain View, California when he was living with his father as a teen.

He also was good in sports; he played football and basketball. He was always excellent in track, just like his mom, he received his high school letter for track in his freshman year. He was good at the long jump especially, and he took many first place ribbons and medals in track meets. He also was a good sprinter. He has gone to college and is pursuing a career as a hair stylist and barber. His motto is to allow him to enhance God's natural beauty. He has many aspirations, and through his faith and belief in God, his dreams will come to pass and his visions will materialize.

My son was in the Navy and went through basic training, he had wanted to work on naval ships but found out he was color blind, so he was only in the service for awhile and came out with an honorable discharge.

He met a very classy young lady when he was twenty years old, she was eighteen and had a two year old son. They married after only knowing each other for three months, needless, to say, they separated a very short time later and they would not have a any contact until more than thirty years later. They didn't divorce, just went their separate ways. He was living in California and somehow through social media, she contacted him and they both were curious and wondered if there could still be a chance of re-kindling the love and salvaging the marriage.

They both decided to meet in Ohio face to face and discuss everything that had happened to each of them in those years they were separated, they tried through counseling to make a go of the lost time, but there were past hurts and present situations that would not allow the re-union to be successful.

He returned to California after a few short months and she decided to move on to be with family out of state.

He is a good father who has learned to be strong, and through mistakes he made in some of his life choices, he knew his children meant more to him than anything else and he began to get go and let God, and once that process started, it was only a matter of time until God stepped in and worked everything out so that he could be a full-time father and through the circumstances, his efforts were not in vain. He kept letting them know that they had a daddy who loved them, and although their parents were not together, they came to a mutual agreement that their children should not have to be without each of them having a part in their development and upbringing.

Jawon, his son, who is now a young man trying to find himself, has made some wrong life decisions which has him in and out of incarceration, at this time. As a child, he was always a blessing, so full of God's spirit. I remember when I first talked to him on the phone, he was just about two years old and so intelligent. He loved music and he especially loved gospel singer; Yolanda Adams. I bought him her music video entitled "The Battle is not yours, it's the Lord's", for Christmas that year, he was so happy and we developed a special bond even then, though it would be years before I would be able to visit California and see my grandson. I pray that he will pull his life together and become the person he is created to be.

He also has a beautiful daughter named Jewel, and she has the sweetest voice, so very soft spoken. She is in college now studying criminal law. Although, I didn't get the opportunity to meet my grandchildren until they were in elementary school, it was as though they had been around me all along. I felt their love and I wanted them to know I would always be there for them; no matter how far the miles, I would only be a phone call away. We had such a grand time in the few days I visited them in California. I had my grandson cooking with me, and my granddaughter would sleep with me at night and tell me how happy she was that I was there. My grandchildren's mother opened her home to me and treated me with much respect and love. She is a good mother, and she taught them to be motivated and to strive to be the best they can be. I came back to Columbus knowing I had grandchildren that lived many miles away, but our love had bridged the distance.

My son is still living in California, and is working as a hair stylist and barber. He was in a long term relationship with a beautiful Nubian queen, Kimberly, she has two grown children which I have met when I went to visit. They became like my extended family. I love them because they are a part of her and she has such a fascinating demeanor.

She has many talents of her own; she is an actress and she has already done numerous plays and is starring in an upcoming movie. I have come to love her already like a daughter. We have bonded so closely, and she really listens to my advice and always asks for my prayers. Although she is suffering with some major health issues, I know God will intervene in the situation and turn her life around for his glory, and she will know that her miracle healing is from God. She shall come through this test and God will get the praise. It is such a joy to see God blessing the two of them and working out the rough edges and drawing them closer to His purpose and plan for their lives.

I love the relationship that God is allowing me with my oldest son. I always knew how much he loved me, but I didn't show my love affectionately as I should have. I thank God He has given me a second chance to express my love to my children openly. I will continue on my life's journey and tell of my relationship and love to my one and only daughter, Pamela, who has always been special to me, although there have been times in her life that she has felt I didn't love her as much as her brothers. She was a precious and beautiful baby girl, even though she was so small at birth, only a little over four pounds, because she was born premature. My mother was so proud of her first granddaughter; she took her everywhere with her and Aunt Dollie became her godmother. With these two women of God to help raise her, she always has had a special spirit.

She never found fault in anyone and always strives to please everyone. She never met a stranger, I was so afraid when she was young that she would get snatched up because she was so friendly. I would tell her don't talk to everyone, but she felt she had to know and make friends with whomever she came in contact with. This trait has proven to be part of her personality and her own ministry. She strived to be a good student and loved music and sports, like her big brother. She played basketball in high school and was the captain of her team. She also ran track.

She has a beautiful singing and speaking voice, which was inherited. She has been in talent shows and has been televised for some of her performances. She also has a gift for teaching young children. She has worked in child care for several years and she has that natural gift for having patience and developing the children's motor skills. Her life has been parallel to my own. She has dealt with some of the same problems that I have gone through, peer pressure, bad relationships, marital discord, financial hardships, stress from children not wanting to obey, and even the loss of a child. She must learn to release things in her life that are delaying her progress, she will have to tune into God's voice as he speaks to her and guides her into her destiny and purpose. Like me, she has gone through a lot of mental anguish and has been diagnosed with bipolar disorder. She has gone through many years of hospitalization and treatment; all of this has taken a toll on her life and has affected her children's lives as well. She is striving to conquer these adversities and build a life of happiness and prosperity for herself and her children. She knows she owes it to them and herself to not give up but keep pressing until her goals are accomplished. She seems to have a hard time of letting go of the people or things that keep coming around to entangle her. Once she learns to not keep looking back and pushes forward, her blessings will come and she will be blessed beyond her greatest expectations.

Chapter 23

MY GRANDCHILDREN ARE my world, and as I speak of my children, I must say something about the blessings each of them has given me through their children. Zakiya, my daughter's oldest child, is in her second year of college on an academic scholarship at the University of Toledo, majoring in Early Childhood as an educator in that field. I am so proud of her accomplishments. It was fun helping her the first year, getting her dorm room set up, and this year she is in an apartment, and once again she has let me and her mom share in helping to put her individual touch on her new residence.

My daughter's oldest son, Kodzo, just graduated from high school this past June and has started college classes at Columbus State University this fall quarter for his associate degree in business. He is studying International Business and may go to Howard University for his major after he completes his associate's degree here. His dad, Kofi, whom I love like a son, has always been in his life and has been instrumental in teaching him to be a strong proud man and to believe in himself and his dreams and to work hard to achieve his goals.

My daughter's youngest son, Kashawn, is fifteen. He is very intelligent also. He is just starting high school, although he is having trouble staying focused in school and is encountering some disciplinary problems because he has been diagnosed with ADHD. I believe he can succeed like his older siblings, but he must want to do all that is expected of him and not to let his behavior keep him from applying himself to the fullest and getting his education and graduating and pursuing his life goals as well. He has proven that he can accomplish these things, because he has been featured in a National Scholastic book called *Who's Who* that honors high school students.

Zyrie is my daughter's youngest child. She has been a joy since she came into this world. She has a special spirit for her age, and she is gifted. I used to put my hand on her mom's stomach when she was pregnant and talk to her and call her my little evangelist. She was born on June 16, and she will be the first to tell you she shares her birth date with the late great rapper, Tupac Shakur.

She loves all music already, but her favorite music is the songs of the late King of Pop, Michael Jackson.

She knows every word of his songs and dances and moves to his beats. She is just six years old, but she is very smart beyond her years and she already has the personality and drive that will accomplish all her life endeavors.

Chapter 24

THE SAME SITUATIONS and demons that tried to destroy me have tried to destroy my daughter too, but I think of where God has brought me from and where He is taking me to, and I get joy in knowing this is only a temporary setback for her comeback, and she shall stand and declare the victory. God has made be know I can do all things through Christ that strengthens me. I trust that the God I serve and believe in has made me able to overcome these negative things in my life, and through a strong prayer life and positive thinking, I have become powerful in my belief and a godly force to reckon with.

I went to work after my divorce; I had never really had to work, so this was strange to have to take on the role of provider and breadwinner. It was difficult, but I got employment as a telephone operator and I worked hard to take care of my young children. They were five and seven years old. We had good times together; we would do things together on the weekends like going to the library and getting books on Black History. I wanted them to know that we are a proud people because we have contributed so much to this nation, and although many things were not taught in school, they could find out on their own through reading and researching. Knowledge is the key to success, and I told my children to always be proud of their heritage and when they grew up to teach their children about our ancestry, so that they too could realize they can achieve their dreams through getting an education and applying themselves to the best of their ability.

There is a section in a song sung by the Father of Soul, the late James Brown, that has been a saying in my life and those words are "Open Up the Door, I'll Get It Myself."

Where and when there is opportunity, we must not be afraid to reach out and grasp the moment, because it may not come again.

My children and I would have fun going to the movies or just staying home and having pizza. I devoted my life to them without a husband until they were in their teens. I had male friends, but I did not disrespect my children's feelings or our home; we had a strong bond of love and trust, and I refused to let that be destroyed by anyone.

Chapter 25

DURING MY CHILDHOOD, I went through many adversities I have tried to block out, but this is the reason for this book to release the pain and nightmares so that there can be complete healing, not just to put ointment on open sores, but to make the scars finally disappear through exposure.

I was six years old when I was raped and molested; this is something you never forget. I thought I had done something wrong to cause this terrible invasion of my small, fragile body. I was a child, innocent and trusting, not understanding how something like this could ever happen. I was so ashamed, not knowing how to let someone know, so I kept this awful secret inside for many years, until I was much older.

My oldest brother was going to Vietnam and we were having a party for him with friends and relatives. I was a young teen at the time and I was dancing and having a good time when this same person that had violated me many years ago made a comment to my mom that I was being too fresh for my age. It was later that night that I confided in my mom the terrible thing this person had done to me. She was so upset that I never came forward earlier with this awful revelation. I told her I was so ashamed that I kept it bottled up inside of me all that time. My mother assured me I did not have to feel ashamed, because I had done nothing wrong to cause this sick individual to take advantage of my innocence and youth.

This is a warning that you must take heed to. Talk to your children, listen to them, watch for any signs that might seem suspicious, gain their trust, and teach them at the earliest age possible the difference between good and bad touching, no matter what or who the person is or whatever they might say to make them feel afraid or threatened. They must feel they can tell you, the parent, anything and know without a doubt you will protect and love them. If the abuse happens to them by a parent or family member, they must tell a friend's parent, a teacher or a minister, an adult they can trust so that the proper authority can be notified.

Chapter 26

MANY YEARS LATER, I went through a period of my life being treated for mental illness. I was diagnosed by a psychiatrist as being bipolar and manic depressive. I received years of treatment and hospitalizations. I was prescribed many different antidepressant medicines, from Lithium to Thorazine. There were so many different pills, I can't even remember the names of all the drugs. I was in and out of hospitals for many years. I even went through a series of electric shock treatments which affected a lot of my memory. I believe it was these undisclosed demons that plagued me since childhood that caused me mental apathy, not chemical imbalance of any brain cells. I have not been hospitalized for over twenty years or taken any of these medicines, and I have gone on to live a normal and active life.

I believe that prayers, not medicine, healed me. I had very low self esteem growing up because I was skinny and underweight, so I was teased and taunted because I was not as developed as other girls my age. I was even told not to cut my hair, which was very long and hung down my back, because this was my best physical asset, and this came from a friend. People don't realize how words can be detrimental to the individual toward whom they aim their bullets of personal dismay.

There was a time in my life that I actually was permissive because I thought this was how a person was supposed to act. The old saying of think before you speak should be embedded in everyone's thought process, like don't say anything if you can't say something nice.

I think because of what happened when I was a child, I was confused for many years about what to do in a relationship.

Chapter 27

I WAS SO in love with Silky Slim, who was the life of the party, I was twenty-three and coming out of a bad first marriage. He would walk into a room and all the women would just go crazy, trying to get his attention. He was a player and I knew it, but he had a way of making you think his feelings were only for you, so never mind the other calls and visits from the other women; he said he was only using them, but he loved me. I loved his family—his mother, grandmother, brothers, nieces, and nephews—and they cared about me too. His mom and grandma tried to warn me, for my own sake, that he wasn't seriously in love with me, he was only out for himself, and of course I didn't want to accept what they were saying. They didn't want to see me hurt.

He had got in trouble while he was in college out of state, and it came back to haunt him. He was arrested for the incident, and when I went to see him at the county jail and he told me he needed me to help him get out of this situation, because once again he made me think I was the one he would come out to, I got him an expensive lawyer who got the case dismissed. I believed he was grateful, but I was fooled into thinking I was the one. I even took him to take his tests to go into the military, and when he joined, I had always thought we would be married, but it was his mom that told me he got married before he left.

I was devastated, but that marriage didn't last. I somehow thought after he came home and we talked, that we still might be together, but he had no intentions of ever marrying me. He married twice after that. I haven't seen him in for many years. The last time I had heard about him, he was still married to his wife who gave him children.

I met Gerry while I was still married to my first husband, but my marriage was already in trouble and I knew it was just a matter of time before we would divorce. I mentioned this relationship earlier but just briefly. Although he was from a different culture and racial background, we shared so many real feelings, and the deep personal interludes that were ours alone would take me through many years of precious memories.We took long walks on the beach and would talk about everything and anything; he inspired me to write my poetry when I was feeling depressed. I would write him love letters and he would write back, even though we were miles apart.

Although I was in Ohio and he was in Pennsylvania, we kept in contact through our correspondence. He would send me letters and pictures, which I shared with my mom because we were close. She commented on how handsome he was, and she wanted to meet him, but she never did.

I thought one day we would break the color barrier and let our love soar, but we lost touch, and after we began to communicate again, many years had passed and he had a family. Young love proved to be just a sweet, forever lasting memory. Our relationship left an impression on my life that I will never erase or forget. Finally, when I moved to California, I met a man who was much younger than me, and we became inseparable; he was more of a friend and confidant than a lover, even though we shared everything. He brought out the best in me, and I was the lady he always wanted to be with. He was an actor, comedian, gourmet chef, and a friend to my sons and family.

We loved the same music like Tupac, Prince, Levert, and Michael Jackson was his idol. We watched the same sitcoms and movies and shared our innermost secret thoughts. Because we would never betray the trust and love, we had years of bliss and unhappiness. I remember we spent New Years in Reno, so it only made sense, after not seeing each other for years, that we would meet up in Las Vegas. I think we created the saying "What happens in Vegas, stays in Vegas," and if we didn't, we should have.

We did everything together. He was full of fun and ideas. He was very creative, even in the small things like going to the racetrack with my sons, who loved him, or twilight fishing to catch shark or other fish and preparing them together, we shared so much. After the meeting in Vegas, he came to Ohio to meet my family, and we swore a bond between us that would never be broken, but it was, and we separated and never really said goodbye. Although we know it will never be again, it is a part of my life I will remember forever, and I will cherish the effect this relationship had on my life. I included this segment in my book to help me understand. I hope anyone else that reads this will know it is better to have loved and lost than to never have known love at all.

Chapter 28

I **MET MY** second husband through my best girlfriend. We were like sisters, always doing things together, working, partying, and enjoying life and everything it offered. He tried to come on like a true player, but deep inside he had a loving and giving spirit. He had gone through a hard life; he lost his father at the hands of a jealous woman who shot and killed him. He grew up bitter, not letting anyone close to his heart, but destiny has a way of being fulfilled, and it brought us together and we shared eighteen years of our lives, married once, divorced twice, and two wonderful sons conceived from this union.

We really had not been together long and I was at work when his brother called and told me what Slim had done; if I had any idea of what he had planned to do, I would have tried to talk him out of this scheme to get quick money. He and his partner had masterminded a bank heist in a small town outside of Columbus. He made history for this crime, because it was the first bank robbery this town had ever had. They had diverted the police by starting a small fire at a school, and when everything was focused on that scene, they had two women go into the bank and get the money. They were almost back in the city before the car used in the robbery was apprehended by the police, and they were captured and taken into custody.

They were charged with bank robbery and Slim was sentenced to prison. He could have done 7 to 25 years, but he did 2 years and 8 months before he was paroled and he never went back to prison for any other crime. His mom and I would go visit him and would take home-cooked meals, like fried chicken or meatloaf, greens, potato salad, and many of his favorite foods. This was before the state penal system did away with this luxury for prisoners because of an increase in contraband of drugs and weapons.

We wrote to each other and kept in touch, but I really had only known him a short time, so I didn't make any promises of waiting for him; I got involved with another man while he was incarcerated. This man was great for me and my kids, and we had a good relationship. I had been still writing to Slim and I made a decision to end the relationship I was involved in and started seeing Slim again, so when he came home we started where we left off, and after three months, on Valentine's Day, February 14, 1978, we got married.

I was working downtown for the local transit company. We went to the courthouse on my lunch break. We were to be married by a judge but we were married by a minister that was on call to the court that day. We exchanged our vows, and I went back to work; I even made it back on time. My co-workers teased me about having the shortest honeymoon in history. Slim always had a side hustle. At that time he would take female friends of his to the doctor and they would get diet pills and he would sell them and give them a few dollars for their trouble. He made enough money that day for us to celebrate our wedding when I came home that night.

He was always making a move to make money; he was a partner with a friend in a clothing boutique. He could design clothes and he looked good in whatever he put on. He was well over six feet tall; everyone called him Slim, and the ladies called him Slim Goodie. He had a beautiful smile and very sexy bedroom eyes, with those long lashes that were the male family trait. All the women would just want to be close to him, but I put them in their place more than once. He loved me and I knew that, so a lot of the other things I just let slide.

Everything went well for a while, but then the domestic violence started. He would hit me and hit me hard, but I would go to work regardless, I would put on make up and cover the majority of bruises and scars. He would be sorry, but I started to do things to get even and he would get mad and we went back and forth. I began to believe this was the way my life was supposed to be. My family told me to leave him and sometimes I would, but I always came back because the love we had was immeasurable and indescribable.

He was always a giving person and he provided me with wonderful material possessions. I think this was his way to show he didn't mean to take me through all the adversity, and he did this to make up for some of the mistreatment.

He was very particular about everything, even more so than myself, so I had to always make sure our home was clean and comfortable. We were both great cooks, so we had a lot of family gatherings, whether it was a boxing party with all the top boxers on pay per view or holiday feasts, the young members of the family always wanted to be around us. He was affectionately known as Uncle Mil, short for Jamil, the Muslim name he took on when he was incarcerated, or Uncle June because he was named after his father. We had moved to Tacoma, Washington in 1979; he was working for my dad at that time, doing some legal business and some illegal business. He got a scholarship to play basketball at a community college and I went to work as an office manager for my father's construction business. I handled the bids for the contracts and took care of the payroll. Tacoma was a beautiful city, with so many parks, and we were having a great life until I found out about his infidelity and drug use, both about the same time. One day he had gone to look for a job and I had decided I couldn't take the misery any longer; I found out he had a mistress that was an airline stewardess and I overheard him talking to her about being pregnant. He told her he would pay for the abortion. He later confessed the relationship, but said it was over.

I was on antidepressant medication at that time. I took an overdose because I wanted to die. I remember getting very sleepy and I felt my body getting heavy; I even smelled the aroma of flowers. I laid back on my bed, and around about this time, I saw my mother's face and she was shaking her head as if to say, "Not this way; you must fight to stay alive." God intervened in this suicide attempt. Right at that time, Slim came home, and when he realized what I had done, he put me in the tub with cold water to revive me and induced vomiting to get the drugs out my system. He told me he was going to call Mom Mabel in Columbus if I didn't come to myself and fight to gain control. I told him I would listen to him, and after awhile I was beginning to feel better, so he didn't have to call the emergency squad, and he made me promise I would never do that again and he would not tell mom Mabel what I had done.

All of this, and then I learned we were having a baby. We had talked about it for a couple of years, and now it was about to become a reality. My sister came to visit me and helped with the baby. She spoiled me with her fresh omelets and all the other good foods she prepared. She decided to stay and start a new life for herself, even after I decided to go back to Ohio, shortly after my baby was born.

My oldest son was thirteen and my daughter was eleven years old when their little brother Jamaal was born. Slim and I always loved Barry White's music, so I think our two sons were conceived while enjoying each other and listening to his love ballads.

Chapter 29

OUR SON JAMAAL was born on April 4, 1980. He came out in a breech position, which meant he was turned the wrong way in the birth canal. He came out bottom first; most babies that are breech usually come out feet first. I looked in the mirror in the delivery room and prayed. I watched as my baby came further down the birth canal; then I saw God had given me my heart's desire: another son. He was so perfect, all ten toes and fingers and a couple blonde strands of hair. Slim and I were so proud; we were both selfish and not wanting to share him. It may have been a parent's intuition that we had to enjoy every second of life with him, and no matter what he did, we cherished each minute and it made the pain more bearable, when the time came and we had to release him back to his creator at an early age.

I got his name, Jamaal, from the Los Angeles Lakers player, Jamaal Wilkes and his middle name from Ahmad Rashad, who played football for the Minnesota Vikings.

Jamaal Rashad made his mark in life. Even if it would be for only a short nineteen years here, he made an impression on everyone who came in touch with him. He had that beautiful spirit and smile that were contagious, and when he walked into a room, his special spirit was felt. As a child he was always trying to please; he was adored by all the family. He had inherited his daddy's smooth demeanor and his grandfather's gift of gab and persuasion. He learned the whole "I Have a Dream" speech by Reverend Martin Luther King when he was in an oratorical contest in Oakland, California at nine years old. He won a gold medal in the citywide contest, in which I still have today, as a keepsake. He loved music and was always dancing. My great-aunt Maude would pay him ten cents to dance for her when he was just two years old. It was such a joy to her; she was in her nineties, and he always made her smile when he danced. He was in rap groups in Oakland, but it was his group "The Little Rascals" that would have an opportunity to audition for the Bobby Womack Production and he met MC Lyte, a famous female rapper and producer during that time. She told him to send her a demo, but we moved back to Ohio when he was twelve, and none of those things ever materialized.

At the age of fourteen, he began to go down the wrong path. He would not listen to authority. Most of his friends were older, yet he seemed to influence their actions; he had started to get involved in gang activity and selling drugs. Weeb was his closest friend and partner. They were like brothers; they were inseparable. They met in the winter of 1995. Jamaal was fifteen years old at the time. He was living on Long Street with his sister, and we had only been back in Columbus for a couple of years after moving from Oakland.

Jamaal had become involved in a lot of street crime activity, and they did many things together, like being in gun battles and gang wars. There were many situations and circumstances that I didn't find out about until after Jamaal died. They were notorious and known in the streets on every side of town and by the law. I remember the first time I met Weeb; he was so respectful and polite to me that I instantly looked upon him as another son to love. It seems like he called me Mom Jackie from the very beginning. He loved our family, and like any son, he protected me, too. I remember once when I was still married to my third husband who had been mistreating me, because when he got intoxicated he would call me out of my name and talk about his girlfriend. Weeb found out and he came running into my apartment and started hitting and beating him because he had disrespected me, and for the way he treated my sons, who were like his younger brothers.

I am still close to Weeb. I still love him like a son. He is serving a sentence of 30 years to life for aggravated murder and robbery. He has been fighting the judicial system on appeals; I visit him every chance I can with his mother, and I will continue to be supportive and show him love. I pray his sentence can some way be reduced and he can come out and be productive and make a positive contribution to the community.

Although Jamaal was arrested and had charges brought up against him on several occasions, he would never see the inside of prison walls, because God had another plan.

I went back to the teachings I had from my mother, and as his mother I never gave up on him and what purpose he was here to do. This is why I know God allowed his life to be taken at an early age so that his soul would be saved. I would pray and anoint his gang flag, as he called it, and I believe through those prayers and some hard knocks he realized this was not his purpose. He started to improve in his school work and had a positive outlook on his life. He was not happy with my life at that time, because I had re-married and I was on the road of my own destruction.

Chapter 30

I **FOUND MYSELF** using drugs and getting addicted to crack cocaine, and he hated my husband for what he had allowed and influenced me to become. This marriage lasted five years, and the whole time he didn't work, because he was waiting on a settlement supposedly for thousands of dollars, because he had got injured on his job before I had met him. I went to work and supported our drug habit, while I was at work I found out he had women in our apartment, they would spend the day getting high and whatever else until I was due home; then they would be gone. He would have the apartment clean and my food cooked, so I wouldn't get upset, but I found out and I did get mad, and I would fight him. He called the police and I got arrested and went to jail for domestic violence. This happened more than I care to remember. I would make bail and in court the judge dismissed the case. I knew I didn't want to keep living a life that was not going anywhere and made me feel so much bitterness and hatred.

Jamaal made me start believing in myself again, I made a change in my lifestyle, the day he called me a crack head, along with the word that means a female dog; this profanity, coming from a son who never had disrespected me verbally, made me wake up and take notice of what this drug was doing to me. I was allowing it to control my life and my children, and even though he sold drugs at that time, I never tried to buy drugs from him, and I know he never would have sold any to me anyway.

One day Jamaal and I were downtown having lunch, and his conversation was that that he wanted his mom back. He wanted me to be happy and to have the smile I used to have and not keep pretending I was happy when I wasn't. It was during these times that I did realize I had to make a choice. I listened to my son, who really not only loved me but adored me; he had a picture of me in his apartment that was taken when I was a supervisor and wore $200 business suits my father had bought me. He was so proud of me, and he was not going to let his mom be the way so many other moms were in the hood. He believed in me, and at that moment I began my recovery; soon after that, I left that marriage and moved in with Jamaal and his girlfriend. They were joyous that I had taken the steps to get my life back on track and to be there to help give my expertise in organizing the apartment and cooking all of his favorite meals.

He went shopping one day and I remember I cooked two roasts for dinner that evening, and none of it went to waste. I found out later, although I had suspected it, that my husband had been having an affair that whole time with his ex-girlfriend, and after I confronted him and her, and almost wrecked my brother's car in the process, I knew I'd been through enough, and I got off drugs.

Chapter 31

I **PRAYED AND** went back to church. I asked God's forgiveness, and He delivered me and set me free from drugs. On January 1, 1999, I called Jamaal to wish him "Happy New Year" and told him I was done with the drugs, and please come get me. He was there in no time and packed up all my things. I never looked back, and I never did drugs after that. We didn't realize at this time this would be our last year--or should I say last few months on earth—together; we became so close, and we had a bond that would never be broken or destroyed again.

I feel God allowed us to save each other. He started going to church with me and he got baptized. He talked about going to culinary school; he was an excellent cook and very creative in the kitchen. Also he had a desire to pursue his music career again. His birthday was on Easter Sunday, April 4, that year and although I had been in a car accident and was on crutches, I managed to cook an Easter feast and birthday dinner with cake included. I didn't know at that time, this would be the last birthday my son would have.

He turned nineteen, and we were all there to help him celebrate: sister Pam and brother Daveron; his girlfriend, Dewana; his niece and nephews, his dad; and a couple of his partners came through and we had a wonderful time; he had a great birthday. James, his older brother, called from California to wish him happy birthday. It was a perfect day. During this time, he was working at a warehouse. He would come in late and I would have dinner in the microwave, so all he had to do was come in and warm it up.

I'll never forget the one night he came in and we had talked for hours and I told him I had to go to work that next day, so he kissed me good night and I went to sleep. The next morning when I woke up. he was on the floor at the bottom of my bed, like he was there to protect me.

We didn't know these moments were going to be some of our last ones together.

His girlfriend had been away for a little while because of some legal problems, but she was coming home, and he was so happy. I had gone to stay with my daughter for a few days to give them some privacy. He would come over, but for some reason he always seemed restless, not his usual self. I would go to sleep at night and I would wake up out my sleep and have strange feelings. I would go on my knees and begin to pray, asking God what He was preparing me for. I didn't know just what was going to take place, but I felt the hand of God strengthening me.

I woke one morning and was getting ready for work. I went downstairs at my daughter's house and Jamaal was there sleeping on the floor. I reached down and touched his hair, gave him a kiss, and left for work. Later that day I called over to my son Daveron's house, and they were playing cards. I spoke to Jamaal on the phone, and he said he was busy, he had to go, but his last words were "I love you." This was April 22nd.

I went to work and after I got off that day, I met my sister, Denise, who was getting married, and we were trying to find the perfect bridesmaids' dresses at the department store where I worked. We shopped and were fortunate to find just the right dresses. I was in line to put them in layaway using my store discount, when I heard her name on the loudspeaker, I thought this was strange and my first thoughts were something might be wrong with Mom or Dad. I hurriedly began to look for her after I left the layaway area, and when I saw her, she was looking at me so strangely. She said she had got a call from Ellis, her fiancé, and said we had to go. I stopped her and I looked at her in the eyes and I asked her three questions.

I said, "Is something wrong with one of my children?" She said yes. I said, "Is it Jamaal?" and she said yes, again, I said, "Is he gone?" and she said yes. I let out a scream so loud that everyone in the store was looking at me. We went to her car and I was in a state of mind I had never been in before. Every time I tried to speak to her, the Holy Spirit would not let me speak in English. I spoke in a heavenly language from the store until we were downtown at Grant Hospital where they had brought my son's body.

I found out he was in the wrong place at the wrong time, and an argument led to a confrontation, which led to a gunshot—one shot in the back, and my handsome son was gone.

I was numb all through those first few days and weeks. I remember the funeral, but everything else was vague. The family and friends came and went. Everyone wanted to comfort me and offer their support and sympathy, but I had to cry out to God, scream silently, die inwardly, pretend to handle it outwardly for my children's sake, but only God could bring me back to reality.

I prayed and tried to compromise, asking God for the answers. I don't remember when, but I do know He made me whole. He renewed my faith and strength, and I was able to live again. I was able to be strong for my sons and daughter. They were hurting so badly too, and we had to depend on each other for strength and to accept what we could not change. I have gone through stories and incidents pertaining to the majority of my life into my thirties, but I must continue so that I can give the whole story behind the glory.

Chapter 32

I **HAVE TOLD** about and described three of the four children I have birthed, so now I will give the history of my last child and definitely Momma's baby boy. My youngest son was born on April 28, 1982, two years after Jamaal. Slim was happy because he kept saying Jamaal needed a little brother because there was eleven years between him and his big sister and thirteen years between him and his oldest brother. Daveron was the cutest baby. He had straight black hair, long eyelashes, and a perfect little round head, and my brother said he looked like a Puerto Rican baby. He was always content, never fussy.

As a child he had ear infections, and the doctors were going to put tubes in his ears because they said this would help his hearing. He had a small speech impairment, but his hearing got better so he did not get the operation, and his speech improved miraculously. He would take his toys and play in a corner for hours, not disturbing anyone. Pam would take care of her little brothers; she was like a second mom. She loved them so much. She was protective of them and devoted a lot of her time to caring for them while I worked and was away from home. Their big brother was a help too, teaching them about sports and other things little brothers needed to learn.

Daveron was very creative; he always had a gift of expressing himself in drawing and writing. He did drawings making tennis shoes that he said he was going to send to Nike Shoe Company, or he would make up cartoon characters. Daveron received an academic achievement trophy in elementary school for writing a short story book. He was also athletic; he started playing little league football at five years old and was really good. I loved going to the field on Saturday mornings after working the third shift at a private residence caring for an elderly couple. I didn't have a car then, so I would catch a bus at seven in the morning and go downtown and catch another bus so I could be at the field by ten to watch him and Jamaal play football with their team, the Hilltop Cowboys.

He was a good child and usually got his way with all the family—after all, he was the youngest. He grew up looking up to his brother Jamaal. They were inseparable, always having each other's back.

They had got mixed up in gang activity and really thought this was their family and they had to be loyal to the gang or die, but they had a praying mother and a mother that knew God would come through, so I would anoint them and pray over them and ask God's protection upon their lives. I remember a time when they had got into a fight with rival gang members, and they told me they had got scars playing rough street ball, but they knew they couldn't really hide the truth from me.

I always told them to tell the truth and shame the devil, so they started to be honest with me no matter what they had done, because that was the only way I could pray and intervene--when I knew what I was up against. The times when they would get in trouble breaking the law, going to court when they were teens, I was there, and because of my presence, the magistrate and prosecutor would be lenient and give them a break. They would let them come home with me; sometimes they were on ankle monitors until their cases were completed. I would tell them this was only going to lead to self destruction and they had too much talent and natural ability they were wasting.

Daveron met the love of his life at age fourteen, and through the years they have stayed together. Their first son was born when they were both just fifteen years old. He has never run from his responsibility as a father and has always provided for his children.

Daveron and Dewana were married July 7, 2007, triple sevens. This was said to be a lucky day because the days only align up like this every hundred years. It was truly a blessed day, and they had a beautiful wedding reception later. They have blessed me with five beautiful and loving grandchildren. They have two sons and three daughters. Daveron, who is only twelve years old, already he is excelling in school, and gearing toward an academic scholarship to Ohio State University. He has been chosen to be in the National Scholarship book of *Who's Who* for his academic achievements. He is a good basketball and football player, too.

Jamaal, his youngest son, that he named after his brother, is gifted as well; he is the quiet one. He loves computers and he can even troubleshoot and repair them, and he is just ten years old. He looks up to his older brother like his dad did with his brother, Jamaal. Jamaal has a disposition much like his dad growing up. He also excels in sports. There is two years' difference in their ages, just like their dad and uncle.

Then there are their three adorable daughters, Alayjah, the oldest, at five is already a scholar and has a mind of her own. She has a fashion sense about clothes and hair. She speaks very fluently and has a way with words. I can see her being a top fashion model or designer.

Jaleah is just three years old and coming into her own personality. She has the sweetest ways and the prettiest smile that just melts your heart and gets her whatever she wants.

Mariah is the youngest of the lot, but surely she is already making her presence known. She is a small and a petite ball of thunder; she is so smart and she is already very alert and discerning. She will be turning two, on June 27th. She checks out everything and everybody and she won't come to everybody or give that beautiful smile to just anyone.

Daveron and Dewana, my daughter in law, whom I love like a daughter, are very good parents; they have survived many struggles, but both of them are strong and God has a calling upon their lives and many blessings in store for them. I hope that no matter what happens, they will continue to let their love grow and pray and look to God. They both are so gifted, and together they can do anything. They have written small children's books and illustrations for their first son when he was born. She is very creative in arts and making things with her hands, and he writes and produces music. They complement each other, and despite becoming parents so young, they have matured into very responsible adults.

Life dealt them a terrible blow, but through everything that has happened, they stand on the word, for what God has joined together, let no man put asunder.

Chapter 33

THEY WERE INVOLVED in a terrible auto accident on November 16, 2006, coming from New York to Ohio. Slim was driving; there was a wreck further up the road, and because of the weather condition, it was a severe storm. The rain was coming down so hard, and as he came off the exit he lost control and hit a large flat bed truck, and this accident took his life. Dewana told me there was such a difference between him and Daveron that day coming back; they were having a good conversation and she said there was a special peace she felt illuminating, as if it was a sign before the accident. They had made this trip before and she said it was definitely not like the other trips they had taken.

Daveron called me at work that afternoon, shortly after the accident had happened, from the accident scene on his cell phone. He was trying to tell me what had happened, he was crying and said, "Mom, I think Dad is dead and Dewana was thrown out the front window." He said his leg felt like it was broken, but he had to be strong and keep it together for Dewana and their daughter.

My little granddaughter, Alayjah, was only seven months at the time and she was in the car seat, but the impact of them hitting the truck projected their van into the air, and she had come out of the car seat and was under the captain's seat.

He was devastated but he kept his composure. I later learned as I got to Pennsylvania at the hospital emergency room with my husband, brother and sister, that my son had not just broken a leg but he was in critical condition and had lifesaving surgery for over six hours and was on life support when we arrived. I also found out that Dewana was so seriously injured going through the windshield that as she lay on that ground with little pulse, he was able to get to her and take a piece of glass from her mouth that was obstructing her breathing to allow her to gasp. When the medics arrived, they thought she was not going to make it, but God was on their side, and while they were rushed to the hospital, our family was in prayer.

My granddaughter was examined but found with no injuries. A miracle took place that day, and they have their own story and testimony. Although Slim has gone on to be with God, his creator, and our son Jamaal, I will always believe their spirit is with us and God has assigned them as our guardian angels.

My son is still undergoing a battle with the court system in New York and even though it has been years now, he was expedited in January 2010, back to New York and he had to do time in Riker's Island in New York. The prosecutor was trying to convict him on charges that carried a sentence of four or more years on possession of a gun with intent. It was through prayers going up from all over the country, that caused a judge to be sympathetic with everything that he had already gone through with the loss of his father and the time that had lapsed; he told the prosecutors he wanted the case done and out of his court, so his defense attorney and the prosecutors did a plea bargain. He had to do six months incarceration with time served. This was about four months at Riker's Island and the rest of his time will be served on probation back here in Ohio.

I have a praise report and a footnote to this situation, on April 13, this year now 2011, my son had to go in front of the judge in New York for a probation violation, and his attorney said he could be looking at more time--between three months up to three years if the judge revoked his probation. Daveron and I made the trip. I was praying for

God's mercy. I prayed all the way there and even in the courtroom. There were prayers going up for him all over the country. He walked up before the judge and when the case was heard, the judge looked at the probation officer. He looked at his attorney and then he looked at Daveron, and he spoke and said, "The probation is terminated."

I showed respect to the court, but I said, "Thank you, Jesus," out loud before we left the courtroom. He does not have to report to New York or Ohio. The battle has been won.

I believe God dispatched His angels to stand beside Daveron in that New York courtroom, and it was a miracle. On the way back he called everyone and told them God had given him not only another chance but a miracle. I saw a real difference in my son's faith that day, and I know he believes now more than ever that prayer is real and God answers prayers. He will be able to continue his youth program that he founded to help inner city youth to divert from drugs and street violence and gangs to become productive in their community with sports activities and other positive programs to build their self esteem and become role models for other youth in their community.

He and his wife have so much to give back to the youth, because they have been together since their early teens and through all the setbacks, they have come out victorious. They still have a way to go, but they are striving to make a difference in their lives and in the lives of those around them.

Chapter 34

I **HAVE SPOKEN** of my second mom, and now I will tell of the ways she and my second dad, her husband, loved me always as a daughter and never as a niece. Mom Mabel is my mom's oldest sister and her husband, Daddy Jack, helped raise me. They gave me all the material possessions like other kids, the things my mom couldn't provide because she was doing all she could raising my younger brothers and sisters. Daddy Jack was a hard worker and he had a good job that allowed him to be able to give Mom Mabel and me a lot of things I never would have had. I was not their biological daughter, but I was their daughter all the same.

My eyes were crossed when I was a child; I had astigmatism and I had to have eye surgery, which they paid for. I've worn glasses since I was two years old. I was supposed to continue to wear glasses after the surgery, but I threw them away after I was growing into being a teenager a few years later.

Daddy Jack was a long haul truck driver and his job took him all over the country, even to Mexico. He would have to be gone for weeks at a time, but he would always call and say how much he missed us. Mom and I would get to travel with him sometimes. I loved being in the big semi tractor trailer and sleeping in the sleeper cab while Dad was driving. He also was a great photographer and he was always taking pictures of the family and the dogs we had as I was growing up.

I would go fishing and hunting with him. He was so special and he always gave me excellent advice as a father, which sometimes I didn't follow, but he was a wonderful father. He never spanked me, only talked to me and told me when I was not being the young lady I was taught to be.

He would bring Mom and me gifts from all over the country. I had real cowgirl boots and hat from Texas; I thought I was Annie Oakley or Calamity Jane. I would play cowboys and Indians with my cousins and brothers. I had a sombrero and dresses from Mexico, and he would also bring hot tamales and peppers. I guess that is why I love hot and spicy food to this day. I had a habit of sucking my fingers when I was little, so they put hot sauce on my fingers, thinking this would make me stop, but I would just lick the hot sauce off.

We always had big family dinners and meals, not just on holidays. We were raised believing in the importance of family. Mom Mabel would cook rabbit and pheasant that Dad would bring home from hunting, and she would fix wild rice and other delicious side dishes and we would have a feast. She was the best cook, and Daddy Jack was a great cook too; he made great spaghetti and pepper steak was his specialty, and it tasted better than any restaurant could make it. My youngest son still talks about Dad's cooking that he remembers enjoying as a child.

I was five years old when my beautiful sister Denise, their daughter, was born. Mom had a daughter that was stillborn that she had before Denise, she named her Yvette Marie.

I loved my little sister so much, and we were always close. I was never considered anything other than her big sister.

Two years later, our little brother Ivan was born. He was my baby; I took him everywhere. I would carry him on my hip and would never let anyone say or do anything to him.

Denise did try to give him food and Kool-Aid in his crib when he was just a baby, but she

was just a baby herself, I just think she didn't want him to cry. We grew up loving each other, and they always considered me as their sister. Since Mom and Dad had them later in life, they were older parents. Mom was there to raise them while Dad was working. Mom was a good mother, but she spoiled them and kept things from Dad because he would be away on the road working. There were a lot of times she didn't tell Dad when my little brother would be bad in school, or later, when he got in trouble with the law.

He got in trouble being rebellious and not listening to anyone. This cost him years of wasted time being involved in crime, including hustling and pimping, drug abuse, robbery, and finally incarceration. Praise be to God and Mom's prayers; God took care of him behind those prison walls, waking and shaking him up. It was there that he realized God's purpose for his life and he surrendered to God's will. He is now an anointed man of God, a warrior, one of God's soldiers who is destined to take the word of God around the world for the healing of souls and preaching the gospel of salvation to the nation. God has given him his mate, his beautiful wife April, and together they are taking their vision to another level, going from the pit to the palace, crossing over from Egypt to the Promised Land. Our belief is before we go to our everlasting home in heaven and our reward of eternal rest, we are going to have God's favor and blessings of overflow here on earth. I am honored to have my brother as my pastor and my sister-in-law as first lady.

There is a story I must tell of a time when we were not in the will of God and I was visiting from California; we were all abusing drugs at that time, but I didn't do drugs with them. It's strange, but even though I got high on the same drug, crack cocaine, I did not feel right getting high with my brother, and I thank the Lord now that I never did. Instead, God used me at a time when I needed some support to overcome my own addiction as well. They had a lot of change they had saved, but there was not any food in the house, so I had an idea to put the change in money wrappers and go to the grocery and get some food. We rolled up over $20, and we put the money in a bag and headed for the grocery. We went shopping and I got some eggs, bacon, bread, coffee, and potatoes. We went back to their apartment and I went to the kitchen and started preparing breakfast from the food we had just brought at the store.

We all ate and started talking, and I believe that God used me at that time even though I wasn't where I should have been in the Lord; I was in a backslider's state of mind, not walking in my purpose, but God knew our hearts and He knew what he created us to be. That night began an escape from that way of life for all of us. I went back to California, and it wasn't too long after that I got a call telling me they were turning their life around and were going to be married.

After a time, they moved to West Virginia and were under Bishop T.D. Jakes' Ministry. My brother studied the word of God and got ordained as a minister in Detroit, Michigan. He moved to Dallas, Texas with the ministry and was the maintenance supervisor over the workers at the Potters House, until God called him to become the pastor over Patmos World Outreach Ministry. He was appointed as an administrator, with his wife working alongside him at a prison outreach center called The Exodus House, in Dallas. It was here God used him to help men and women coming out of prison to get back into society and become positive and productive individuals in their community.

I have always been close to my brother and I secretly prayed that he would bring his ministry back to Ohio, so when my sister-in-law told me God was telling them they needed to come back home it was really no surprise, just my prayers being answered. Mom and Dad were getting up in age and their health was failing; they had been down in Texas with him for seven years, and so the decision was made for the family to move back.

Mom and Dad came first and stayed with me and my husband Mike until we found an apartment for them close to our home, while Ivan finished up business in Dallas preparing for the move here. Mom was glad to be back home so she could be close to Aunt Audrey, her only living sister. Aunt Audrey has always been the quiet but strong woman of God; I have always admired her, because it seems as the road of life got tougher, she just kept getting stronger. It has been good for the two of them, and they have always enjoyed being over to my house together, so they can spend quality time with each other.

Dad, on the other hand, was not really content; he loved the weather in Texas, so he wasn't happy with the move back to the snow and cold. I tried to appease him and make all his favorite foods like liver and onions, spaghetti, and beans and cornbread during the winter. I know if he had his way, I am sure he would have stayed in Texas.

We were taking Dad to his doctor visits and the doctor said he was developing dementia. They felt he showed symptoms of Alzheimer's, and he began taking medicine to help his memory loss. Dad was so sweet during his last years. He never complained; there were times when we knew he wasn't well, but he didn't say anything, except he still had his sense of humor and we would enjoy him telling stories. The grandchildren all loved to be around him. He was in the hospital once when the family was there and he started imparting words of wisdom to each of us; we all sat there in awe, knowing he was getting close to his transition. His words were inspirational, and they seemed to come right from him communicating with God. It was like in the biblical time when an elder was dying; he would call his loved ones and give his blessing and pass the mantle to the next in charge.

Daddy Jack and I had a special connection all the way back; when I was a little girl and he and I would go the park and he would take pictures of me and our dogs. He was always there for me, advising and showing love as a father. They don't come better than him anywhere, and I am so proud that I had him in my life. I was at the hospital with Daddy Jack when he took his last breath and the angels came to escort him to his eternal home in heaven. Ivan did Daddy Jack's eulogy like no one else could. God gave him strength to perform this task and the home going for Deacon Carey, our father, was a praise service.

I had co-workers that are very dear friends, Michelle and Sharon, that came and said they had never been to a funeral service such as this, and when my brother gave an altar call they felt the spirit of God.

I wrote a poem in Dad's remembrance and his granddaughters, Ivory and Ivana wrote beautiful poems too for his service. My sister Denise has taken his death so hard; she has not been the same. I know she was her daddy's girl and she can't let go just yet and just think on the memories that are there for her and know she is blessed to have had such a wonderful father.

Daddy Jack has been gone for two years, but his memory will be with us until we meet him on the other side.

Daddy Jack lived to be ninety-five, and we thank God for every year we were blessed with his presence. Mom and Dad were married over fifty years, and they instilled in us their values and quality of life, to know we can trust in God and He will bring us through every trial and storm.

Chapter 35

I HAVE BEEN blessed to have the favor of God that has allowed me to have the kind of influence from my parents to build a personal relationship with God and to know I can conquer all tribulations through unwavering faith and belief. I want the world to know God has brought me a mighty long way, and He is not through with me yet. I have been able to look adversity in the face and laugh at the tricks that satan has put in my path to try and persuade me to turn around, but I have come too far to not go all the way and see what the end is going to be. I believe my latter years will be my best years, and I will be able to leave a legacy for my children and grandchildren to be proud of. I have only briefly mentioned my loving husband of ten years, Michael, but our love and marriage definitely must have a part in the finalization of the purpose of my life's story.

I have a wonderful husband who is also my closest friend.

We have gone through many trials and tribulations, but it has only made our love stronger. He is an excellent provider; he works so hard to give me everything that he even thinks I might need. He has always been a workaholic, and he is a perfectionist in his job performance. I met Michael about two months after Jamaal died. I had just moved to up north to an apartment and was living with my son, Daveron, Dewana, and my grandson, Daveron. I was working at Value

City department store as a traffic coordinator for the warehouse. I had been employed there for about two years. I was going through work issues in regards to my attendance because I just couldn't seem to get things together because of grieving Jamaal's death. I had stopped in a local family owned gas service station and was talking to the owner, whose family was very nice, and I had shared with them some of my story as to why I had moved to the neighborhood and they had welcomed me to the area. I would stop in after work and get me a Pepsi or something for my grandson before I walked home, which was only about a quarter of a mile up the road.

It was during one of these times as I was talking to the owner that this young man walked in with the keys to a white convertible Mustang that belonged to the store owner's daughter. He casually spoke, and I could tell by his speech that he had a southern accent. I later learned he was born in Tennessee. He was friendly, and as I started to walk out of the store he asked me if I would like a ride home. I accepted only because I felt I would be safe, because he knew the owner of the store, who he seemed to give his approval, and he was in a work uniform with his name on it. I thought it was unlikely that I would have any trouble, and besides, it was only up the street where I lived and it was day time.

He went around to the passenger's side to open the door for me. I was very impressed, and when he started up his car, he was listening to gospel music. I thought to myself, I was going to be alright for the short ride home. We talked quite easily, and the conversation was light. He did ask me for my phone number; I gave it to him and politely thanked him for the ride. He got out and opened my door again. I said goodbye and he left.

It was about two weeks and I had gone back by the store, and it was the store owner's daughter that told me he worked behind their store and was a car detailer. He had done her car that day when I met him and was just dropping it back off. I said he asked for my phone number but he hadn't called. She gave me his last name and the name of the company he worked for. She said if I just asked for Superman, they would know who I was talking about.

I went home and called the company and asked for him. I was a little nervous. I didn't want him to think wrong of me, but I did want to get to know him better. He came to the phone, and when I told him who I was he seemed surprised, but he asked if he could come over after work that evening and of course I said yes. It was around six when he knocked at the door. My son and his girlfriend were there, and my little grandson. I introduced him and then they went back to their room to give us some privacy. He was very polite and he had asked if he could bring something to drink. I told him yes, but I had said I don't drink but he could bring me a pop and I never told him which pop was my favorite. He had a beer for himself and he brought me a Pepsi—yes, my drink of choice.

We talked and were able to determine we did want to see each other again.

We began to date. This was in June of 1999 and by October he asked me to marry him. I said it was too soon, but I had fallen in love with him too, so we decided we would wait but not a real long engagement.

We married the next year on September 9th. This was a good day. It was also my uncle Elmer's birthday, my mom's oldest brother. He was still living then and he had met Michael and he liked him, so I felt this was a good sign. We had a small, intimate wedding with a few family members and friends at my Aunt Dollie's house. She is an ordained minister and she performed the wedding ceremony. We went on a cruise to the Bahamas and Cayman Islands for our honeymoon. It was so beautiful and romantic; it felt like a storybook fairytale, but this was real, a dream come true.

I thought I could never love like this again, because I had been hurt and I was very protective of my feelings, but I began to love and trust again, and although as in any relationship we have had problems, but we have learned to communicate and always try to understand what the other is feeling. We had a small business, but because of economic hardship we had to file bankruptcy and lost our home to foreclosure, but I did not lose my faith and I remained faithful and continued to honor God with praise and tithes, and within two years of this devastation, God was showering us with favor.

My husband has gainful employment with a company that is located in several states. He is a manager and he is in a better financial position than he was before. We are buying a second home on land contract and I have a brand-new car, and he is driving an SUV that is fully loaded with a DVD player and On Star navigation and satellite radio. He is starting our detailing business again and doing mobile service for his customers.

He only had one offspring, a lovely daughter, Qiana, that has blessed us with two more precious grandchildren. Our granddaughter Zuri just turned three years old and she has just went through bone marrow transplant; now we must wait and pray that the transplant will allow her better health and she can live a long and productive life. She is getting stronger every day and her immune system is building back up. Our grandson Jaiden turned a year old in November. He is a happy child. He is always smiling and is a papa's boy and he looks a lot like his grandpa Mike.

I have become very close to my stepdaughter's maternal grandparents; they are very caring people and they have been a blessing to us and to Qiana, their granddaughter, and the great-grandchildren as well. My husband has not always been able to express his love toward his family as he should, but God has given him a new perspective on the importance of family ties, and now we are sharing closer times with the family. We had a big Thanksgiving at our home with his family members for the first time, and we had a wonderful time.

My mother-in-law is happy that he has found someone that loves him unconditionally and works with him to have something in life. She has been there for us when things were down and gave a helping hand to assist us, along with other members of his family, to show us love and support. My father-in-law also is a loving father, and he is proud of our accomplishments. He is still living in Tennessee with a daughter and granddaughter, and they come to visit when they can. I feel God has given us favor, and it's as if we have an invisible force field around our relationship. Nothing is able to penetrate through or destroy the love we have built up. We have mutual respect for each other's feelings and interests.

My husband can play drums and he was in a gospel group that had a CD out years ago. Hopefully, he will find the time again to use his talents for the glory of the Lord. He has aunts and uncles who are renowned gospel performers, ministers, and pastors. As I write this story, many of our loved ones are leaving this earthly domain and putting on their heavenly attire. In the last two years an uncle, two cousins, and now my precious Daddy Jack have gone home to glory.

The scripture says being absent from the body is being present with the Lord.

I will keep pressing toward the mark of my higher calling in Christ Jesus.

Chapter 36

I HAVE NOW lived to witness the first African American President of the United States of America. I was able to be a part of this nation's history when I attended the inauguration on January 20, 2008 in Washington, DC, of the swearing in to office of Barack Obama, the 44th President of the United States. I was able to witness the harmony of diversity, and we were all able to feel a strength and warmth in spite of the weather, which was cold and below freezing on this eventful day that made the thoughts and words of the late Reverend Martin Luther King come alive. He said he had been to the mountain top, and his "I Have a Dream" speech is becoming reality.

These last two years have been a struggle for our nation, trying to recover from the worst economic times since the Great Depression. We will see a brighter day, and as I watch my grandchildren growing up, they can dream and achieve anything they put their mind to, with strong determination and education--yes they can, and yes they will.

I am thankful that God is using me to make a difference in others' lives through just a word of encouragement or a prayer that they can overcome through faith and a desire for a closer walk with God.

I have gone through physical and mental abuse, rape, domestic violence, mental breakdowns, suicide attempts, drug abuse, and so many pressures that should have taken me out or to my grave, but I have come this far by faith, and through the prayers my mother prayed and taught me to pray, faith will lead me home.

God has given me His favor and I will forever keep the faith.

www.ingramcontent.com/pod-product-compliance
Lightning Source LLC
Chambersburg PA
CBHW060440090426
42733CB00011B/2351